Christina Faescher

After all this time...
Goodbye!

AF191454

Über die Autorin:

Schon als Kind war Christina Faescher fasziniert davon, wie gut man Gefühle in Form eines Textes ausdrücken und vor allem verarbeiten kann. Angefangen mit Songs und dann Gedichten, wagte sie sich anschließend an Kurzgeschichten.
Ihr Traum war es damals schon, irgendwann ein Buch zu veröffentlichen. Und manchmal werden Träume wahr.

Christina Faescher

After all this time…
Goodbye!

Impressum:

Copyright: 2024, © Christina Faescher
Verlag: BoD · Books on Demand GmbH,
In de Tarpen 42, 22848 Norderstedt,
bod@bod.de
Druck: Libri Plureos GmbH, Friedensallee 273,
22763 Hamburg
ISBN: 978-3-7693-5633-5

Bibliografische Informationen der Deutschen National-
bibliothek: Die Deutsche Nationalbibliothek
verzeichnet diese Publikation in der Deutschen
Nationalbibliografie; detaillierte bibliografische Daten
sind im Internet über www.dnd.de

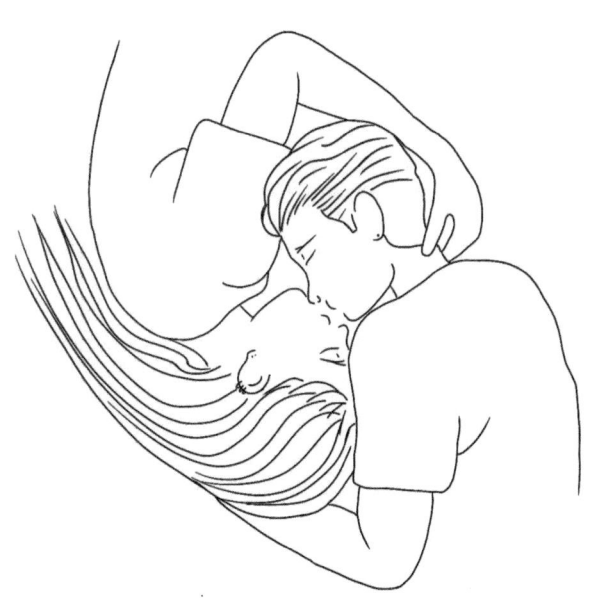

Take a paper, take a pen.
Write down your pain the best you can.
It will help you, you will feel,
how deep inside, you'll start to heal.

This is for you...

READ IT HOW YOU WANT TO

There is no right order to read the poems.
You can read it from top to bottom, from bottom to top, or criss-cross.
Because just like every street has its curves, healing has its ups and downs. It's not linear.
Sometimes I loved you the most in the middle of the heartbreak.
And hated you deeply when I was right at the urge of forgiving and forgetting you.
But someday there will be no ups and downs, there will be no curves.
Because this street will be gone. Just like my pain and my love for you.

MOON

Every day at 9 p.m. I look for the moon and hope you do too.

Maybe us both looking at the moon at the same time is the closest we can ever be without hurting each other.

I MISS YOU

It's been over **14 months** since we last talked.
And I still miss talking to you and I miss your voice.

It's been over **64 weeks** since we laughed together.
And I still miss the sound of your laugh and the
wrinkles when you smile.

It's been over **445 days** since we saw each other.
And I still miss your eyes. Your eyes were able to see
right into my soul.

It's been over **10.680 hours** since we kissed.
And I still miss the way your tongue would make me
feel and I miss your bitter taste every now and then.

It's been over **640.800 minutes** since we were close.
And I still miss the feeling when your skin touches
mine.

It's been over **38.448.000 seconds** since you held me.
And I still miss the way you would make the world stop
just for this moment.

But it's been **0 days, 0 minutes, 0 seconds** since the
last time I thought about you.

PRETENDING

You didn't love me.
But you loved you.
Or you pretended to.

I didn't love me.
But I loved you.
Or was I pretending too?

I CAN'T LET GO

I loved you. I loved all of you. Every single version.
And that's why I couldn't let you go.
When you left, I thought I would die.
I lost every hope and joy. And it got really dark.
It's not like I wanted to kill myself.
I just wanted to fall asleep and never wake up.
See I had to let go of you.
So, I let go of the love I had for you.
But the hate stayed. Now I can't let go of the pain.
Because that's all that's left. And I am not ready for that.

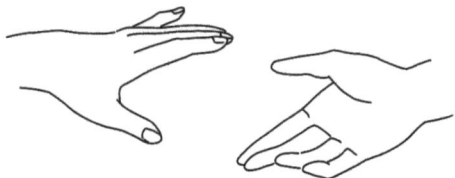

I USED TO

I used to love you.
I used to want to spend every second with you.
I used to cry and miss you.
I used to forgive you.
I used to want you back.
I used to hate you and talk bad behind your back.
I used to protect you still from every snitch.
I used to hate it when you tell people lies about me
like I'm the witch.
I used to hate that you were better at this game on this
battlefield.
But my side of the story doesn't matter anymore
because
I have healed.

I USED TO (PART 2)

I used to love you and talk to you.
I used to care.
I used to kiss and touch you all the time.
Then you left. We stopped talking and kissing.
I thought the breakup was the worst part.
I thought the world would stop.
But it didn't.
And as time went by, I stopped loving you.
I stopped caring.
I stopped to remember how it was to be with you.
And the worst part is, someday
I will stop remembering you at all.

I CHOSE YOU

I chose you.
I chose you over and over again.
I chose you on your darkest days.
I chose you when you didn't show love.
I chose you when you lied to me.
I chose you when you cheated.
I chose you when you wouldn't even choose you.
And I hoped that someday you'd wake up and choose me even for one day.
But you didn't, so I woke up and finally chose myself.

MY FAVOURITE MEMORY

You becoming just a memory
will always be my favourite memory
and the best part of us.

TIME

I think somewhere at the beginning of time.
We were one, like two sides of the same dime.
Like two pieces of the same soul.
Just when we collide, we feel whole.

But somewhere not right at the beginning of time.
I think someone committed a crime.
And put a spell on you and me.
That we attract and repel for eternity.

So time after time, while after while.
I'm still into you; I'm into your smile.
I hate what's inside but do love your style.
But I only love you when you are not mine.

And as time went by, I lost you, out of sight.
And I lost you out of mind, right until tonight.
We are like the moon and the sun. Yes, they both shine.
But rarely meet each other and that's perfectly fine.

YOU'RE EVERYWHERE

I'm in my bed, you're not here.
I'm in my head, you're everywhere.

A THOUSAND LIFES

I wish, you would have never left me.
Cause then I would have never stopped loving you. I would have never stopped seeing you through red coloured-glasses.
But you did. And I did.
And I have realised that we are so different. We don't have the same values. And now I wonder how we made it that far.
I know that even if I would die a thousand times we wouldn't end up together.
Even if we get a thousand lifes to try and make it work we wouldn't be a match.

WAS IT ALL IN MY HEAD?

I still don't know what this was.
When you were fake and when you were real.
Or was it all in my head?

I MISS THE FAKE YOU

Seeing you would always make my heart beat faster.
Touching you and feeling your lips on mine was always
the best part of my day.
And now that we're done, my eyes are always looking
for you no matter where I go.
My lips are craving for you. My whole body misses you.
I miss you. The fake version of you that I created in my
mind that was never really you.

ELENA AND DAMON KIND OF LOVE

I always wanted the Elena and Damon kind of love. A love that is full of emotions. And that is worth fighting for. A love that is everything but boring.
But then I realised that this love is a big red flag screaming at the top of their lungs. This love is full of pain and anger and self-doubt and manipulation. And maybe even hate.
This love can't be boring. It's full of ups and downs, full of thousands of emotions. This love isn't stable: it's dangerous. This love is a constant heartbreak and in the end you even stop loving yourself.
So no. I don't want this kind of love anymore.
Because this isn't even real love. It's obsession, attraction, and most of all it's addiction. To the stress and the drama.

And this is exactly what we had.

I'M SORRY

I'm sorry that I loved you too much and you weren't there yet.
I'm sorry for not seeing the signs you gave me. Maybe I didn't want to see them.
I'm sorry for all the hurtful things I said to you and most of all I'm sorry for all the things I said about you.
I'm sorry that I couldn't give you the time that you needed and wanted.
I'm sorry for outing you, just to hurt you.
I'm sorry for every pain I've caused. On purpose or not. I'm truly sorry.
I'm sorry I couldn't be the best version of myself.

And I also forgive you.
I forgive you for every lie, every hurtful thing you did, every cheat, every game you played.
I forgive you for coming back multiple times just to leave me again.
I forgive you for taking my friends and making me look bad after the split.
I forgive you, that you couldn't be the best version of yourself.
I forgive you all.

And I wish you the life that you deserve.

HOPE

In a different life,
a different earth
or somewhere in the multiverse,
we might have worked.
And hopefully, we get the happy ending
I always wanted us to have.

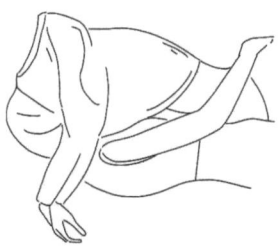

Take me into your world under your shirt.

YOU AGAINST ME

I thought it was you and me against the world but it
was me
against it all. And you against me.
But now that you're gone, it's me and my inner peace.
I came to ease, thank you for the release.

YOU WERE MY DRUG

When I think of you, I think of love.
Not because I loved you deeply. I think of love because I realised that what I felt and what we had was so far away from it.
It wasn't love: it was attraction, affection. And most of all, it was addiction.
With you I had higher highs than any drug could have given me. But also the lowest lows.
And after some highs and lows, the highs didn't felt high enough. But the lows felt even lower.
But I still wanted to feel it every time I got the chance to. Until I didn't. So I got sober.

SHOOTING STAR

When we first met, I saw a
shooting star and made a wish.
I wanted you to kiss me.
I thought it was romantic.

But I didn't know that a shooting
star is just a rock or dust that gets
on fire as soon as it enters our
atmosphere and burns down.

Just like I did. As soon as you
kissed me, you set me on fire
until I burned down and died inside.
You were the orbit I should have
never entered.

I DON'T MISS YOU

I don't miss you.
I don't miss the pain that you caused. I don't miss being
lied to and cheated on. I don't miss the disrespect.
But I do miss our rare moments full of passion.
When we weren't talking.
When our eyes locked and our hearts melted. When the
world stood still and your heartbeat became mine.
When our souls started dancing and our lips moved to
the beat.
I miss those moments.
Right there, right then, you were the love of my whole
existence.

THIS ONE SONG

Your lips on mine were magnetic.
We could kiss for hours and hours. We kissed through
every show and every movie. We kissed to every song.
Except one.
Cause one day this song will be the one I will dance to at
my wedding.
So I skipped this song every single time we were
together.
This song belongs to my future wife only.
And deep down, I knew that it will never be you.

YOU BROKE MY HEART

You broke my heart. But it didn't stop you.
So you broke my soul, my self-esteem, and self-love.
And then you left 'cause there was nothing else you
could destroy.
You never wanted to see me cry.
You wanted to see me lying on the floor, dead inside.

ROSE-COLOURED GLASSES

Sometimes I forget how much you hurt me.
How much I hate you.
But I do remember how much I loved the person you
could've been.
I loved you, because I saw so much potential in you.
I believed in you.
But then again, maybe I just saw you through rose-
coloured glasses.

THE PROBLEM

The problem wasn't that we didn't loved each other enough. Or that I loved you too much or you didn't loved me at all.
It wasn't that simple. But then again, it was.
Because…
The problem was we loved differently but wanted to be loved the same.

I'M BETTER WITHOUT YOU

I thought you were the one.

I loved you with all my heart. But then you left.
And it took me a while to realise that it was the best
thing that happened to me.

'Cause over time we became so toxic to each other.

And I can only be the best version of myself when **you**
are not a part of my life.

THIS WAS LOVE

And maybe...
just for a second...
we both thought that this was love.

YOU WERE MY TYPE

You were my type.
My type isn't brunette or blonde or red.
My type isn't black.
My type isn't smart or funny or driven.
My type is a red flag.
So... yeah...
You were my type.

YOU LOVED THE GAME

We used to work together.
You used to write to me. More and more.
You used to call me during the day and then in the
middle of the night.
And I always picked up. Because I liked you. Maybe a
little more than I showed.
You asked me to pick you up 'cause you were drunk.
And I did. I drove you home.
And then we started to hang out with each other.
And I started to fall for you. And you started to fall for
this game.
And then we kissed. You left your taste in my mouth.
And over time, I wasn't falling anymore.
I loved you. And you...loved the game.

WE WERE NEVER MEANT FOR EACH OTHER

From the moment I saw you, I pictured our life together.
And when we started dating, I thought about how many kids we would have, where we would live.
And when you left I realised, that I loved the version of you I created in my mind.
The real you and the real me were never meant for each other.

HEARTBREAK

I thought you could hear the heart break. I thought it was just a moment. It takes just a second.
But it isn't and it doesn't.
You broke my heart over a period of time. And while my heart is healing now, it still breaks whenever I see you or find out about another lie you've told me.
My heart is healing and still breaking at the same time.
And maybe it will never be the same.

REPLAY

If I could push rewind, I wouldn't change a thing.
I would replay every single second the exact same way.
But I would throw away the tape.
Because it reminds me of the person I once was.

I BELIEVED IN YOU

I wish somebody would've told me that loving you
would destroy me.
That your love wouldn't be real. And that you
wouldn't only break my heart but also my soul, my
spirit, and my mindset.
I wish somebody would've told me that laughing with
you one minute would mean crying the next.
But then again, I saw the red flags. All of them. Right
away.
I saw the red flags in every move you made and every
word you said. I saw them every time I caught you
lying.
I definitely saw them when you hurt me and made me
feel like the villain that had to apologize.
Yes I saw every red flag. But I chose to ignore them.
Not only because I loved you. But because I believed in
you.

I AM THE LOSER OF THIS GAME

If our split had been a game, I would have been the loser and you the winner.
But not because I've lost something great and you've dodged the bullet.
I loved you. And after the split, I was so full of pain, I was hurt and so angry. So I talked bad about you.
But you never loved me. That's why it was so easy for you to make it look like I was the villain and you were the victim.
So yeah. You are the winner and I am the loser of this game.

THE WAY WE WANTED TO BE LOVED

When we met, I knew you weren't ready to love me the way I wanted to be loved.
And after we broke up, I realised that I never loved you the way that you wanted to be loved.

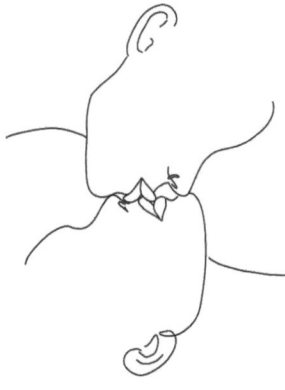

I DESERVE BETTER

You took everything from me.
You took my team that I liked.
You took my job that I wanted.
You took my friends that I needed.

But you can have it all.

You can have that team that you turned against me in a
heartbeat. 'Cause someday, someone will turn them
against you as easily.
You can have that job that would have made me sick
because of all the gossip. And someday, we both know
it, it will make you sick too.
You can have those friends of mine that were unloyal.
So now you all can be fake to each other.

You can have that.
You can have that all.

'Cause I deserve better.

FINAL BREAKUP

You hide and you lie.
I find out and I cry.
We fight and we break up.
Just so we can make up.

And then we repeat.
But different indeed.

You lie when you say you like me.
I cry 'cause I feel you don't.
We make up and I try to ignore it.
Till we break up 'cause I couldn't.

And we're back to repeat.
Again different indeed.

Everything you say, it's just a lie.
You cheat on me, you make me cry.
You don't want us and neither do I.
I don't want you and me, I want a You and an I.
We still make out, but we don't make up.
Yes, this is our final breakup.

JUST A TOY

When I met you, I wanted to be with you so badly.
And I thought you wanted to be with me too.
And when I started to fall in love with you more and
more. When I wanted to spend every second with you
and give you my all. You started to lose interest in me.
Instead, you started to see us as a game. I became a toy
to you. You wanted to see how often and how far you
could throw me away. And you loved to see me running
back to you every time you gave me the chance to. And
I would always come back to you. But with time you
got bored. You played all the games you could think of.
You threw me as far away as you could. It got old. I
turned into this old doll you didn't want to play with.
You needed new toys. And all I wanted was for you to
come back to play me one last time. To hold me one last
time. Even for a second. Cause I still loved you. I loved
you through it all. And when I loved you the most, you
didn't want me at all.

DARKNESS

You were my favourite person. Your love was my
favourite drug. And you were my daily routine. You
gave me purpose and structure. You were my first
thought when I woke up.
I would write you good morning. Write 1.000 messages
throughout the day. Talk to you on the phone and see
in person. I would touch and kiss you and breathe you
in.
I would even see you when I closed my eyes. And when
the day turns to night, you were my last thought. I
would write you good night or fall asleep with you on
the phone.
And then you left. I lost my favourite person, my
purpose, my structure, and my daily routine. My
favourite drug was gone and I had to get sober
overnight.
When you left, you left me with nothing.
You left me with darkness.

ROCK BOTTOM

You broke my heart.
Tore me apart.
Tried to make me drown.
Flipped my world upside down.
So I hit rock bottom, lost my feet off the ground.
My heart got silent, but my head got loud.
I wanted to kill myself, 'cause the darkness got bigger
And my life turned to hell so I pulled the trigger.
But I think I've dodged the bullet twice, 'cause I got the
right back-up.
Yes, I hit bottom, but I got right back up.

OUR SIDES ARE EQUALLY IMPORTANT

You have your side of the story and I have mine.
But the truth is, we both are wrong.
Because it didn't happen like you said it did and it
definitely didn't happen like I said it did.
And maybe it wasn't even somewhere in between.
Still, your side of the story is important and so is mine.
It is based on our emotions and experiences we made
through time. With each other. With others.
Our stories are equally important and both, true and
false. All at the same time.

THANKS TO ME

I used to laugh at people who said they wouldn't change
a thing because that made them who they are.
Until I met you.
You broke me and hurt me in the worst way.
But I healed my broken heart, and I worked on all the
traumas that would lead me to people like you. 'Cause,
honestly, I don't want to end up with people like you.
Ever. Again.
So, yeah, I wouldn't change a thing because this made
me who I am. I am stronger and wiser than I ever was
before. But I'm not gonna thank you for teaching me
this lesson.
I thank me for doing the hard work and learning from
it.

GREATEST LESSON

I always thought that you were my biggest blessing.
But I've realised that you were my greatest lesson.

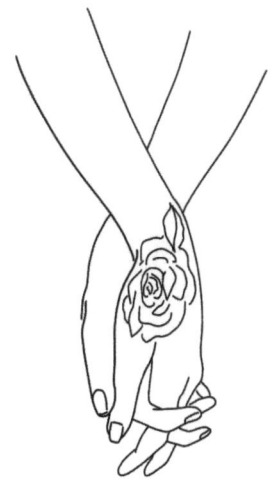

YOU WERE MADE FOR ME

Nobody understood what you meant to me.
You weren't just somebody. Just a girl that broke my heart.
You were so much more. See, I was never myself before you broke me. When I dated my first girlfriend, I just figured out that I'm into girls. I was on a journey to find myself. And when I met my second girlfriend, I was depressed and broken because I just lost my mother. When she broke my heart, I worked on myself 'cause I knew I never wanted to date someone like her again. I became confident. I found myself. And then you came. I was so blown away. But you tore me apart. You showed me my spoiled roots. And for the first time I saw the problem. I attracted the same girls because this toxic love was all I knew. It was all I saw when I was a kid. It felt familiar. So I knew I had to break the circle so history won't repeat itself. I understood that we weren't made for each other. But you were made for me.

DOING THIS FOR ME

I'm not writing this for you.
I'm not doing this because you were something big or
special.
But my feelings for you were.
And they deserve to be let out.
To be set free and to be mourned about.
I'm not doing this for you.
I'm doing this for me.
And eventually **I'm doing this for her**.

HELLO

If I would have known that loving you would mean losing me, losing the best version of myself and forgetting how to love myself, then I would have left at hello.

DON'T MATTER ANYMORE

All the love notes I wrote.
They don't matter anymore.

LETTING GO

I'm letting you go.
But whenever I see a white car,
I make the same wish.
I wish, you'd come back.

I'm letting you go.
But whenever I see a shooting star,
I make the same wish.
I wish, you'd come back.

I'm letting you go.
But whenever I lose an eyelash,
I make the same wish.
I wish, you'd come back.

I'm letting you go.
But whenever I see the clock strikes 11:11,
I make the same wish.
I wish, you'd come back.

I'm letting you go.
But whenever I see the moon,
I make the same wish.
I wish, you'd come back.

I'm letting you go.
But whenever I hear a joke or a word
that reminds me of you,
I make the same wish.
And when I see something or someone
that reminds me of you
I wish you'd come back.

I'm constantly wishing you'd come back.
But I'm letting you go.
This is my final goodbye.
And as much as I wish you'd come back.
I wish you stay where you are.
Cause that means I stay happy.

I'm letting you go.
And I stay happy.

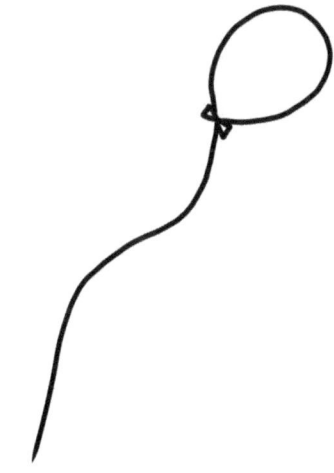

GOODBYE TO THE ERAS OF US

From strangers then friends who had some fun.
To the girl of my dreams, you were the one.
From all love and I love all about you.
To the conversation we had, they were all about you.

From the secrets we had to I guess we lied again.
To just tell them you love me if you're gonna lie again.
From being drunk in love until I was undrunk.
To the heartbreak you caused and feeling stung.

From I love you bitch till you screwed behind my back.
To I'm a better version without you and I don't want
you bitch back.
From the silence between us to sex with my ex.
To the things we said about each other behind our
backs.

I loved every version of us but what's even more bitter
You're not just a serial heartbreaker, you are a quitter
But it's ok, I don't hate you, cause if I hated you.
I couldn't let you go and would always be bound to
you.

I let you go but I'm still healing from us.
From every single one of the 7 eras of us.

Yes, I loved you through every season of us.
But now it's time to say goodbye to the eras of us.

Shhh...
don't say it

I'LL BE FINE

Before you my life was perfectly fine.
But then you came and our path became one line.
But maybe it was me who didn't see the sign.
That our life's they never did combine.

Like a crossroad. Your life was only crossing mine.
Like in an X. It only meats one time.
There's no next but I swear that I'll be fine.
Till then I drown my sorrow in red vine.

BREATHE AGAIN

A breakup is like breathing after a long run.
It feels like you can't breathe. Everything is hurting.
But after a while you calm down and start
breathing peacefully again.
That's the time you actually looking forward to run
again.

NUMBER 8 IS FOREVER

You were number 7.
7 is my favourite number.

And you were my favourite person. But also my biggest enemy. You made me feel like heaven. But also made me feel like hell.
See, 7 stands for wisdom, which I gained thanks to you.
It stands for a big shift that impacts your life and you did.
7 stands for two goddesses: of war and protection.
Or love was both. Our battlefield and our safe place.
And still we lost.

Now I'm waiting for number 8.
Because 8 is forever.
We weren't made for each other. You never meant to stay.
But number 8 is forever.

AFTER ALL THIS TIME … GOODBYE

This book is a piece of my heart that I'm ready to let go of.
So…
After all this time… Goodbye!

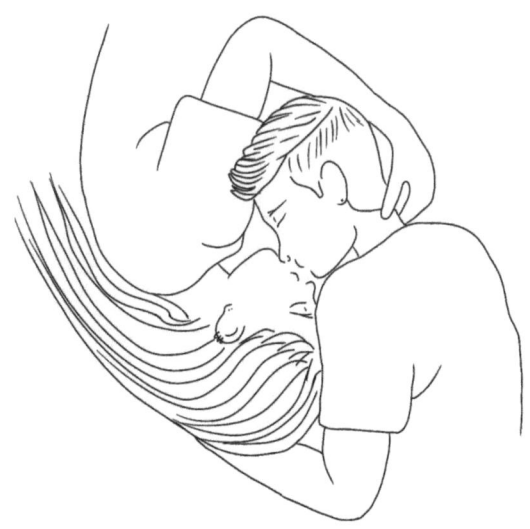

This is not for you...

FRIENDSHIP

We had a friendship that could have been terrific.
It was all there. The bond and the laughs. And „we stick
together till the end". But it was only me.
I was all in.

I stayed by your side when no one else did. And I
fought for you when you couldn't. But you chose to let
me down.
You chose to cheer up that one person that broke my
heart.
So I left.

And when you came back and wanted to be friends
again,
I knew that you lost one of the truest friends that you
had.
I just lost someone who didn't even care when I was
broken and sad.

ARE YOU WORTH MY TIME?

There are so many people in this world. Not everyone will like you. No matter what you do and who you are. So, don't waste your finite time and your energy to please them. Maybe you're just not their cup of tea and they are not yours. Learn to let go of these people and everything that isn't good for you. That's how you make space for people who are worth your time.

I WANNA THANK ME

I wanna thank me
for getting out of bed even though I wished I never
woke up.

I wanna thank me
for always trying to kick back when depression kicks in.

I wanna thank me
for taking help and not be embarrassed about it.

I wanna thank me
for keep fighting and never getting tired of it.

I wanna thank me
for being alive.

I wanna thank me
for always trying to smile even though the clouds are
right above me.

I wanna thank me
for not crying because life is tough.
Life gets tougher when you cry.

STOP CRYING

When everything around you falls apart, stop crying. You can't save anything when you drown because of your own tears.

IT WILL GET BRIGHTER

When everything is dark, it will get lighter.
And in this darkness it will shine even brighter.
The smallest dot will shine brighter than a star.
It takes time but you won't be forever where you are.

Thank you for this therapy session.

DANKE

Danke, an jedem Einzelnen, der sich mein Jammern angehört hat. Immer und immer wieder.
Danke, dass ihr mir gezeigt habt, dass ich nicht alleine bin und dass es doch noch tolle Menschen auf der Welt gibt.

Ich war oft überrascht darüber, wie viele gute Seelen da draußen sind. Man erkennt es meistens nur, wenn man positiv und offen dem Leben gegenüber tritt. Verbreitet weiterhin das Positive, ihr macht die Welt zu einem besseren Ort.

Danke auch an all diejenigen, die mich bei meinem Projekt unterstützt haben und mir geholfen haben, es zu Ende zu bringen.
Manche gaben mir bei Cola und Kuchen hilfreiche Tipps und haben mir bei meinen Entscheidungsschwierigkeiten geholfen. Danke nochmal dafür. :)

Danke, dass ich bei euch immer ICH sein durfte.

Bei diesem Buch ging es genau darum. ICH zu sein.
Meinen Gefühlen Raum zu geben und heilen zu können.

INHALT

Das ist für dich...

DU BIST

Du bist viel mehr als das, was du von dir hältst
und weit mehr als das, was andere von dir halten.

MANCHMAL

Manchmal verletzen wir Menschen, weil wir Egoisten sind.
Und manchmal verletzen wir Sie, weil wir uns nicht trauen, wir selbst zu sein.

Wir wollen allen Menschen gefallen, suchen Bestätigung und wollen in die Gesellschaft passen. Also fangen wir an, uns zu verstellen und unterdrücken, wer wir wirklich sind. Wir sind lieber unbeachtet zwischen allen anderen, anstatt wir selbst auf unserem eigenen Weg. Doch vielleicht sollten wir mal versuchen, unsere Masken abzunehmen und es wagen, uns zu zeigen? Denn es wäre doch ziemlich enttäuschend, Gott gegenüber zu sitzen und zu realisieren, dass wir das einzige Leben, was wir haben, für andere gelebt haben. Was wäre das für eine Verschwendung? Also lasst uns unseren eigenen Weg frei wählen, weniger auf die Meinung anderer hören und aufhören, Angst zu haben, dass unsere engsten Menschen uns nicht mehr lieben werden. Denn wenn sie uns wirklich lieben, wird diese Liebe nur noch intensiver. Denn wie viel näher kann man sich schon kommen als sich demaskiert in die Augen zu gucken?

Ja… Manchmal hinterlassen wir unsere Spuren auf dieser Welt und manchmal hinterlassen wir sie auf den Herzen der Menschen, die wir einst geliebt oder verletzt haben.

ICH WÜNSCHTE

Ich wünschte, wir könnten die Zeit zurückdrehen.
Zu dem Tag zurückgehen,
an dem wir uns das erste Mal sahen
und noch DU und ICH waren.

Ich würde die Freude aus meinem Hallo nehmen,
die Lippen nicht zu einem Lächeln heben.
Ich würde dich wahrnehmen, aber nicht sehen
und meine Welt würde sich weiterdrehen.

PLAYLIST

Unsere Geschichte war ne Playlist, wo nur der Anfang
richtig rockt.
Und mit jedem nächsten Song, machte es einfach
keinen
Bock.
Angefangen wie ne Party, lass uns jubeln, lass uns
schreien.
Und enden melancholisch, lass uns gehen, lass uns
weinen.

ES GEHT MIR GUT

Alles, woran ich denken kann, bist **immer nur du**.
Du bist jeden Tag auf replay, da ist **niemand wie du**.
Bei jedem Lächeln tobt ein **Schmetterling** in meinem Bauch.
Wenn du die Augen schließt, spürst du das auch?
Du bist schöner als ein Stern oder **1000 Sterne**.
Ich verliebe mich in dich, es ist mehr als hab dich gerne.
Du verdrehst mir den Kopf, doch **dazwischen sind wir Freunde**.
Doch dann fällt der Kuss zu meiner großen Freude.
Ich muss dich **tausendmal** küssen, **immer wenn wir uns sehen**.
Dich **1000 mal** spüren, bevor wir wieder gehen.
Zwischen meinen Zeilen versuch ich dir zu sagen:
Ich liebe dich. Und du? Doch trau mich nicht zu fragen.
Geb dir den **kleinen Finger schwur**, ich werd dich niemals hassen.
Werd dich für immer lieben. **Wenn du mich lässt**, dich nie verlassen.
Ich dachte, ich bin **perfekt für dich**.
Doch wir sind es nicht.

Wir sind wie **20 Tage Regen** ohne Sonne, die dann scheint.

Wir sind die **Mutprobe**, die keiner schafft und dann weint.

Wir sind das **Gewitter, jede Nacht** überschwemmen wir den **Fluss**.

Wir sind getränkt in Gift und töten uns aufs Neue bei jedem Kuss.

Wir sind das **Auf und Ab**, das **eigentlich, vielleicht**.

Wir sind **schwarz** und niemals weiß und es ist niemals leicht.

Wir sind wie **Kopf aus** in 'nem Krieg mit **100 Tausend** Toten.

Du hast recht, auf eine andere Art, ist unsere Liebe verboten.

Und dann war es aus.

Du gingst aus meinem Leben raus.

Es ist **vorbei**. Ich bin der **Verlierer**.
Ich hab die **Liebe verloren**. Doch bitte **sag nie wieder**:
„**Ich hoffe, es geht dir gut**. Dich zu verlieren tut mir
weh.
Doch du findest **jemand anders** und es **tut nicht
mehr weh**."
Du warst von Anfang an ein **Arschloch**, ich hab es
nicht gesehen.
Hast mich belogen und benutzt und ich wollte mit dir
gehen.
Ich wollte doch nur, dass du mich liebst.
Mir nur ein kleines Stückchen von deinem Herzen
gibst.

Du warst alles, was ich wollte, du in meiner Nähe.
Doch du hast dich gesehnt nach einer fremden Nähe.
Von einem Mann, einer anderen Frau.
Ich wurde niemals aus dir schlau.

Ich frage mich was mich geritten hat, denn vor Liebe
war ich blind.
Nun **vergiss mich**, lass mich gehen. Deine Liebe ist wie
der Wind.
Immer in Bewegung. Bleibt nie an einem Ort.
Ja, **es geht mir gut**, denn du bist nun hinfort.

Das war für all die Herzen, die vor Schmerzen brennen.

Ich riech nicht mehr nach Keller,
doch du riechst noch nach Pfütze.